# The Will of God

# The Will of God

## LESLIE D. WEATHERHEAD

ABINGDON PRESS/NASHVILLE•NEW YORK

# PREFACE

Here are five talks on the will of god, given to my City Temple congregation. My friends the Rev. Edgar C. Barton and the Rev. Leslie F. Church thought their publication might help others to clarify their minds on a subject that is specially relevant to these days of loss and sorrow. I have left them in the direct style in which they were written down, and have not attempted to disguise the fact that they were prepared as sermons.

L. D. W.

# CONTENTS

# 1

## GOD'S INTENTIONAL WILL

The phrase "the will of god" is used so loosely, and the consequence of that looseness to our peace of mind is so serious, that I want to spend some time in thinking through with you the whole subject. There is nothing about which we ought to think more clearly; and yet, I sometimes think, there is nothing about which men and women are more confused.

Let me illustrate the confusion. I have a good friend whose dearly loved wife recently died. When she was dead, he said, "Well, I must just accept it. It is the will of God." But he is himself a doctor, and for weeks he had been fighting for her life. He had called in the best specialists in London. He had used all the devices of modern science, all the inventive apparatus by which the energies of nature can be used to fight disease. Was he all that time fighting *against* the will of God? If she had recovered, would he not have called her recovery the will of God? Yet surely we cannot have it both ways. The woman's recovery and the woman's death cannot equally be the will of God in the sense of being his intention.

Let me illustrate the confusion again. "My boy was killed ten days ago in one of the raids on Berlin," said a woman, "but I am trying to bow to the inscrutable will of God." But was that the will of God? I should have said it was the will of the enemy, of Hitler, if you like, of the evil forces we were fighting. Are they then the same thing?

Here is a mother wringing her hands and weeping in anguish because her baby is dead. Her minister stands by her, longing to comfort her; but though his presence and prayers may offer consolation, he knows only too well that when the storm is raging it is too late to talk about the anchor that should have been put down before the storm began. What I mean is that it is so important that we should try to think clearly before disaster falls upon us. If we do, then in spite of all our grief we have a philosophy of life that steadies us as an anchor steadies a ship. If we do not, the storm is so furious that little can be done until it has abated. If only the minister could have injected into the mind of the woman his own belief about God! But that, alas! is impossible. In her anguish, this is what the woman said: "I suppose it is the will of God, *but if only the doctor had come in time he could have saved my baby.*" You see the confusion of thought. If the doctor had come in time, would he have been able to outwit the will of God?

The matter came to me most poignantly when I was in India. I was standing on the veranda of an Indian home darkened by bereavement. My Indian friend had lost his little son, the light of his eyes, in a cholera epidemic. At the far end of the veranda his little daughter, the only remaining child, slept in a cot covered over with a mosquito net. We paced up and down, and I tried in my clumsy way to comfort and console him. But he said, "Well, padre, it is the will of God. That's all there is to it. It is the will of God."

Fortunately I knew him well enough to be able to reply without being misunderstood, and I said something like this: "Supposing someone crept up the steps onto the veranda tonight, while you all slept, and deliberately put a wad of cotton soaked in cholera germ culture over your little girl's mouth as she lay in that cot there on the veranda, what would you think about that?"

"My God," he said, "what would I think about that? Nobody would do such a damnable thing. If he attempted it and I caught him, I would kill him with as little compunction as I would a snake, and throw him over the veranda. What do you mean by suggesting such a thing?"

"But, John," I said quietly, "isn't that just what you have accused God of doing when you said it was his will? Call your little boy's death the result of mass ignorance, call it mass folly, call it mass sin, if you like, call it bad drains or communal carelessness, but don't call it the will of God." Surely we cannot identify as the will of God something for which a man would be locked up in jail, or put in a criminal lunatic asylum.

THOSE who want a text for this sermon will find it in the eighteenth chapter of St. Matthew's Gospel and the fourteenth verse: "It is NOT the will of your Father which is in heaven, that one of these little ones should perish."

We see by these illustrations—which, of course, could be applied to other disasters besides death—how confused and loose our thinking is about the will of God. But let me here at once relieve the tension of your mind by anticipating some of the things that I want to say in subsequent sermons of this series.

My own thinking demands a division of the subject into three parts, the first of which we are discussing:

1. The intentional will of God.
2. The circumstantial will of God.
3. The ultimate will of God.

The trouble arises because we use the phrase "the will

11

of God" to cover all three, without making any distinction between them. But when we look at the Cross of Christ, we can see, I think, the necessity of such a distinction.

1. Was it God's intention from the beginning that Jesus should go to the Cross? I think the answer to that question must be No. I don't think Jesus thought that at the beginning of his ministry. He came with the *intention* that men should follow him, not kill him. The discipleship of men, not the death of Christ, was the intentional will of God, or, if you like, God's ideal purpose —and I sometimes wish that in common language we could keep the phrase "the will of God" for the intentional will of God.

2. But when circumstances wrought by men's evil set up such a dilemma that Christ was compelled either to die or to run away, then *in those circumstances* the Cross was the will of God, but only in those circumstances which were themselves the fruit of evil. In those circumstances any other way was unworthy and impossible, and it was in this sense that our Lord said, "Nevertheless not what I will, but what thou wilt." Because a father in the evil circumstances set up by war says to his son, "I am glad you are in the Army, John," it does not mean that from the beginning he willed the Army as John's career. The father would much have preferred, let us say, that his son should be an architect. The father wills the Army for his boy only because *in the circumstances which evil has set up* it seems to the father, and, indeed, to the boy, the most honorable, as well as inevitable, thing to do.

3. Then there is a third sense in which we use the phrase "the will of God," when we mean God's ultimate goal—the purposefulness of God which, in spite of evil and, as we shall see, even through evil, arrives, with nothing of value lost, at the same goal as would have been reached if the intentional will of God could have been

carried through without frustration. I hope we shall come
to see in the other sermons of the series that God cannot
be finally defeated, and that is what I mean by his omnipotence—not that everything that happens is his will,
but that nothing can happen which *finally* defeats his
will. So, in regard to the Cross, God achieved his final
goal not simply in spite of the Cross but through it. He
achieved a great redemption and realized his ultimate
will in as full a sense as he would have done if his intentional will had not been temporarily defeated.

I know people's minds are very tired through war
strain and weariness, but I do want to ask you, in view of
any possible hour of subsequent sorrow or disaster, to try
to hold in your mind those three distinctive ideas which
can finally be harmonized, but which, for clarity, we do
well to hold separately: the intentional will of God, the
circumstantial will of God, and the ultimate will of God.

So WE concentrate on the first and think of the will
of God in the sense of his ideal intention. To accomplish
that, one of the first things we must do is to dissociate
from the phrase "the will of God" all that is evil and unpleasant and unhappy. That we shall deal with under
the heading "The Circumstantial Will of God." The
intentional will of God means the way in which God
pours himself out in goodness, such as the true father
longs to do for his son.

In this matter see how confused our thinking has been
made by bad hymns. Here is a verse from one of them:

> Though dark my path and sad my lot,
> Let me be still and murmur not,
> But breathe the prayer divinely taught,
>     "Thy will be done."

What sort of a God is this, who of his own *intention,* not through circumstances thrust into life by ignorance, folly, or sin, but of divine intention, pours misery undeserved and unhappiness, disappointment and frustration, bereavement, calamity, and ill health on his beloved children, and then asks them to look up through their tears and say, "Thy will be done"? We simply must break with the idea that everything that happens is the will of God in the sense of being his intention. It is *within* the will of God, if you must use the phrase, in circumstances we have hinted at already. But we must come to terms with the idea that the intentional will of God can be defeated by the will of man *for the time being.* If this were not true, then man would have no real freedom at all. All evil that is temporarily successful temporarily defeats God.

To go back to our earlier illustrations, I could not say to my dear friend, "You wife's death is not the will of God at all. It is the fruit of human ignorance, and if we could spend as much on medical research as we spend on a battleship, your wife's life could have been saved"; but though it was not the right moment to say it, one could not help thinking it.

When a young missionary declares his readiness and determination, having been thoroughly tested, and having passed all the necessary examinations, to give his life in order to bring the good news about Christ to people who have not heard it, then we may truly say, "Thy will be done." Not when an airman is brought down in flames to meet an untimely death, but when the war is over and the young men of all nations can shake hands and begin together to build a new world—that is the time to say, "Thy will be done." Not when the baby is dead, but when two young people take their little one before the altar to dedicate him or her to God because they want

God to be enthroned in their lovely little home and in the new life that has been born to them—that is the time to say, "Thy will be done." Not when little children starve in Europe because of the circumstances of war which the evil of the whole world has brought into being, but when Europe is delivered at last from the ruthless heel of the oppressor, and all little children in a United States of Europe have enough to eat, and can sing and play again happily in the sunshine, with fit bodies and fit minds— that is the time to say, "Thy will be done."

Come with me to some slum home in the dark back streets of a huge city, where men's lives and services are means to other men's ends, where there is disease of body and distortion of mind, where evil festers and grows in sordid and terrible conditions, where men have not even the spirit to rebel, but accept their lot with a listless apathy that is more terrible than a revolution. And if you say concerning those stunted lives, "This is the will of God," I say to you that that is a greater blasphemy than the denial of the Holy Trinity. Industrial oppression, selfish greed, the denial of God's gifts to his own children because of the greed of the few, the horror of war—these things spell a greater atheism than any verbal arguments man has devised. We turn back a hundred years and wonder that Christian men could sing hymns to God while slavery was rife. But, please God, a hundred years hence our descendants will turn back and become incredulous that we ever called ourselves by the name of Christ when his body was torn asunder in our churches, trampled on in our streets, exploited in big business, left to disease when medical knowledge and skill were within reach of the human family, and mutilated by the bombs and burning steel we dropped on one another's cities. Call these things evil, call some of them inevitable evil because of widespread sin, but don't call them the will of God.

Do you not see, therefore, how important it is that we should get our thinking right about the will of God? For by our confusion we thrust people's minds into unbelievable torment; we blunt the edge of social purpose until men mutter the slogan, "God's will be done," when the very opposite of God's will is being done, and when, if men had seen more clearly into the divine purpose and tightened up their loose thinking, they would have become the instruments of God's purpose and swept away the evil which they complacently regarded as the will of God. Men have chanted the phrase "the will of God" as savages chant incantations, sealing the whole subject with that silencing taboo and evading the challenge of the disturbing questions which honest thinking would have set ringing through their minds with the insistence of a trumpet call.

THERE are, however, two difficulties:

1. The first might be put like this. You may say, "Yes, that's all very well, but people get a lot of comfort from supposing that their tragedies are the will of God. One can bear a thing if it is God's will. It is hard to bear it if it is a ghastly mistake and not the will of God at all. Your view is robbing men of comfort. When they feel a thing is the will of God, they can bear it with equanimity."

I am unrepentant. Admittedly there is a time when things can be said and there is a time when they cannot be said, however true they may be. If you are standing in the presence of some great tragedy, there is very little you can say about the will of God. But I would go on immediately to add this: There is never any final comfort in a lie. However closely we may have hugged a lie to our bosom, the moment we see it to be a lie, we should be wise to part with it. Those who take refuge in a lie are like those who take refuge in a flimsy storm shelter made of three-ply wood painted to look like stone. When they want the shelter most, it will let them down. He who hides in an idea about God which is not true will, in the hour of real need, be left as comfortless as atheism would leave him; and if it is his own refusal to think things through which lands him in a flimsy shelter that can never give his soul any strengthening protection, then the refusal to think is sin, for Christ commanded that we should love him with all our mind. I know that to face the truth is costly, and people hate to be made to think, but only the truth can set us free.

2. Second, there is another objection which could be expressed thus. A man might say, "It is all very well to keep the phrase 'the will of God' for the lovely, joyous, healthy, beneficent things that happen to people; but surely some of the greatest qualities in people are made by suffering, and therefore is not that suffering the will of God? For example," this objector might say, "look how the war brought courage to men and women." This we will discuss more fully as we think of the circumstantial will of God, but let me make some reply to the objection.

There is a bad snag in the logic of the objector's remark, for he cannot go on to say, "Therefore the war was the will of God." The war did not *make* courage. It revealed the courage that was there all the time. It gave it a tremendous opportunity for self-expression. Evil is never creative of good, though the circumstances of evil have often been an occasion for the expression of good.

Look not only at the flaw in the logic but at the false implications for theology. If we say that the suffering caused by evil is essential because of the qualities evoked, then logically we must assume that God needs evil to produce good: that he could not produce such a thing as

17

courage unless an evil like war demanded it; that when Jesus healed men he was defying the will of God instead of doing it, in that he was removing something essential to the growth of the soul. If that is true, what happens in the heaven of heavens after all souls are gathered in at last? Will all the qualities which evil reveals atrophy into nothing because there is no evil to evoke them? I repeat that evil does not *make* good qualities. It *reveals* them and gives them exercise, but there is always the possibility—and surely this is God's intention—that those same qualities may be revealed and exercised and manifested as a response to goodness.

Let me recall to you in this connection the words of Jesus: "O Jerusalem, Jerusalem, which killeth the prophets, and stoneth them that are sent unto her! How often would I have gathered thy children together, even as a hen gathereth her chickens under her wings, and ye would not! Behold, your house is left unto you desolate." Note the words "ye would not." They imply, "Ye might have done." Or look at some other words of Jesus: "If thou hadst known in this day . . . the things which belong unto peace! but now they are hid from thine eyes." Note the words "If thou hadst known"; they *might* have known, then. The grand qualities in human nature are not given birth by evil. God creates them, and they are sometimes revealed by the right reaction of the good man to evil, but they do not depend for their origin on evil, for they *can* be evoked by a response to the good.

Let us be very, very careful how we use the phrase "the will of God." I should like in closing this section to make reference to the passing of a very great religious leader, the Rev. Dr. F. Luke Wiseman. On a dreadful, foggy day this old saint of eighty-six preached twice— once in Wesley's own pulpit in City Road. Then the old man made his way home. His wife died many years ago.

18

His family are all grown up. We can imagine the old man sitting down in his armchair by the fire. He went to sleep and awakened in heaven. About that you can use the phrase "Thy will be done"—and some of us would add another Biblical phrase: "May my last end be like his."

We will later fit calamity and distress into the framework of our thought about the will of God, but in the meantime keep the phrase for God's intention. And when you see his glory reflected in this lovely earth, in nature around us so full of his beauty, in poem and song, in picture, in music, in great architecture and in lowly service, in the lives of lovely people, in the happiness of a home, in the health of the body and the resilience of the mind and the saintliness of the soul, then, looking up to your Father in heaven, say, "Thy will be done"; and let us so dedicate ourselves that we may be made one in the glorious harmony of all things and all people who carry out his will, that it may be done in earth as the angels do it in heaven.

# 2

# GOD'S
# CIRCUMSTANTIAL WILL

WE SAID THAT THE PHRASE "THE WILL OF GOD" IS used so loosely as to land us not only in a confusion of mind but in a torment of feeling.

When a dear one dies, we call it "the will of God," though the measures we used to prevent death could hardly be called fighting against the will of God, and if they had been successful we should have thanked God with deep feeling that in the recovery of that dear one his will had been done. Similarly, when sadness, disease, and calamity overtake men they sometimes say with resignation, "God's will be done," when the opposite of his will has been done. When Jesus healed men's bodies and gladdened men's lives in Palestine, he was doing the will of God, not undoing or defeating it.

We therefore divided our subject into three as follows:

1. The intentional will of God—God's ideal plan for men.

2. The circumstantial will of God—God's plan within certain circumstances.

3. The ultimate will of God—God's final realization of his purposes.

Once again, even at the risk of being tiresome, let us look at the supreme illustration of the Cross.

1. It was not the intentional will of God, surely, that

Jesus should be crucified, but that he should be followed. If the nation had understood and received his message, repented of its sins, and realized his kingdom, the history of the world would have been very different. Those who say that the Crucifixion was the will of God should remember that it was the will of evil men.

2. But when Jesus was faced with circumstances brought about by evil and was thrust into the dilemma of running away or of being crucified, then *in those circumstances* the Cross was his Father's will. It was in this sense that Jesus said, "Not what I will, but what thou wilt."

3. The ultimate will of God means, in the case of the Cross, that the high goal of man's redemption or, to use simpler English, man's recovery to a unity with God—a goal which would have been reached by God's intentional plan had it not been frustrated—will still be reached through his circumstantial will. In a sentence, no evil is finally able to defeat God or to cause any "value" to be lost.

LET us now concentrate on the second of these divisions and speak about what I call "the circumstantial will of God." We may make the matter clearer still by restating an earlier illustration and thinking of a father planning his boy's career, in co-operation with the boy himself. The will of both may have been, let us say, that the boy should become an architect. Then comes the war. The father is quite willing for his son to be in the armed forces; but a Navy, Army, or Air Force career is only the father's interim or circumstantial will for his boy, his will in the circumstances of evil which war has produced. It would only be confusing to speak as if the father's ideal intention and original plan for his son was that the latter should spend valuable years of his life in the armed forces.

Now in the same way there is an intentional purpose of God for every man's life; but because of human folly and sin, because man's free will creates circumstances of evil that cut across God's plans, because our oneness with the great human family means that the evil among other members of it may create circumstances which disturb God's intention for us, there is a will within the will of God, or what I call "the circumstantial will of God"; and in the doing of that the soul can find peace, the mind can find poise, and the will can be so expressed that ultimately the original plan of God is brought to successful fruition.

I think there are two parts to the circumstantial will of God—one in the natural realm and the other in the spiritual.

1. Let us look at the Cross of Christ again. Given the circumstances of evil, it was God's will that Jesus should be betrayed, taken, crowned with thorns, crucified, left there in the blazing sun to die. The laws of the universe, which are themselves an expression of God's will, were not set aside for Jesus, the beloved Son. The laws which govern the hammering in of nails held on the day of Crucifixion in just the same way as they do when you nail up a wooden box. If bombs are dropped from an airplane over the closely built dwellings in a city, they pierce the roofs of the godly and of the ungodly; and if nails are hit with a hammer wielded by a strong arm, they pierce the flesh even of the Son of God; and because the laws of the universe are operating, and because those laws are an expression of God's will, you may, if you like, call these things the will of God, but only in the limited sense described. The forces of nature carry out their functions and are not deflected when they are used by

the forces of evil. Those who lost dear ones in recent wars will not need me to say more about that. When Christ's flesh was lacerated on the cross, the laws of God in regard to pain operated just as they do when we get hurt; and Christ accepted that as part of the ordering of the universe which was the will of a wise, holy, and loving God. He did not fling it back at God that it was unfair that the laws should operate in his case because of his character.

2. But there is a second element within that circumstantial will of God. The first we may call natural, the second spiritual. Christ did not just submit to this dread event of the Crucifixion with what we miscall "resignation." He took hold of the situation. Given those circumstances which evil had produced, it was also God's will that Jesus should not just die like a trapped animal, but that he should so react to evil, positively and creatively, as to wrest good out of evil circumstances; and that is why the Cross is not just a symbol of capital punishment similar to the hangman's rope, but is a symbol of the triumphant use of evil in the cause of the holy purposes of God. In other words, by doing the circumstantial will of God we open up the way to God's ultimate triumph with no loss of anything of value to ourselves.

Now let us turn from the Cross and see this truth in a very human illustration. Take the case of the unmarried woman in middle life whose mind has almost closed against the probability of marriage. What was once an eager expectancy becomes a hope growing dimmer and dimmer, and then dying away. Now it is not the intentional will of God that she should remain unmarried. The divine intention, surely, is that every woman should have a home and a husband and babies. The very structure of her body and the creative centers in her brain, her sex instinct and her maternal impulse, are sufficient evidence of this, for every woman possesses all these things. Though some instincts can be repressed into unconsciousness, or can be diverted into nonbiological activities, every instinct is present in every person, and biological fulfillment is God's intentional plan.

But supposing that the tyranny of evil circumstances —and they are evil if they deprive women of their primary *raison d'être*—thrusts a woman into a dilemma. She cannot have that part of her nature biologically satisfied, let us imagine, unless she sacrifices her ideals—cannot have sex without sin. Then the circumstantial will of God is that she shall remain frustrated, and that circumstantial will can be looked at from two angles. It falls into two parts—one natural, the other spiritual.

First, there will be a physical sense of sex starvation, for no so-called sublimation completely solves the difficulty here. Sublimation is always a second-best for the time being. But, second, she must not merely resign herself, perhaps with bitterness, to the unmarried state, but must react so creatively and positively to God's circumstantial will that she makes something glorious out of life which God can use for the fulfillment of his ultimate will, namely, to make her a complete and integrated personality in union with himself.

We note, then, that the second part of God's circumstantial will cannot be done without human co-operation. Without that, the Cross would have been another in the long list of capital sentences carried out by a savage and barbarous state. It would have been a noble sacrifice for an ideal. In the case of the kind of woman we have described, without cooperation the woman would simply resign herself to the forces of the universe and make her frustration unendurable. She has to find by a positive and creative attitude to the situation—which, be it noted, evil, not God, has thrust upon her—the circumstantial will of

24

God in it, so that out of the frustration she may make an immense contribution both to her own inner harmony and to the final purposes of God. This, in fact, is what many women have done. Sublimation is easier to talk about than to accomplish. It is particularly easy for those who do not have to practice it to talk about its value for others. Actually, it is not technically sublimation until it becomes unconscious—until, that is to say, our instinctive energies are running in a nonbiological channel without our realizing the fact at all. But sublimation may well begin by directing the activities of the personality to some altruistic task which is (a) of use to the community, (b) satisfying to the self, and (c) in harmony with that self's ideals. Only under those three conditions can effective sublimation be realized.

The common illustration is work among other people's children. But in doctoring, nursing, craftsmanship, music, writing, organizing, running clubs and other people's homes, women use up the energy in ways helpful to the community, satisfying to themselves, in harmony with their ideals; and in so doing they extend immensely the kingdom of God.

In parenthesis, one ought to add that nothing could be more cruel or heartless or stupid than to sneer at the unmarried woman in middle life. It is especially intolerable when such a sneer comes from those who are married for no reason for which they should be proud. All who work among the people will report that wherever unselfish service for others is being carried on at a sacrifice of personal comfort, there the unmarried woman in middle life will be found, serving the community and forcing the circumstances of evil that have frustrated God's intentional will to contribute to the achievement of his ultimate plan.

I can imagine such a woman saying, "I know that the will of God was that I should express my nature as other

25

happily married women do, and of course I should love to have my own home and family. But I am not just going to let the universe get me down, for there are no circumstances which God allows that can finally defeat the ultimate purpose which he wills; and as Jesus reacted to the circumstances of evil and thereby turned his crown of thorns into a crown of glory, and his cross into a throne, I can take hold of these circumstances and win something from them that will bring harmony to my own nature, which will contribute to the happiness and service of the world, and which will further the kingdom of God."

No one, you see, can say to God: "Well, of course I wanted to do this and that, but I was the victim of illness or sorrow or frustration or war or death or loss. So what could I do?" For there are no circumstances which will be so deadly as those Christ had to face. No possible situation can ever arise which *of itself* has the power either to down us or to defeat God—no, not even death. For although thousands of deaths happen that are not the intentional will of God, he is not beaten by any possible juxtaposition of circumstance. Probably death, and therefore the fact that we serve him in heaven instead of on earth, does not make more difference to the ultimate plans of God than whether we serve him in London or Manchester.

One thing *is* incredible, that God should allow circumstances to happen which inevitably defeat his ultimate purposes. If he did, it would mean that he had abdicated from the throne of the universe, whereas the truth is that, though the revolt against him seems formidable, "the Lord God omnipotent reigneth." As the writer to the Hebrews said, "We see not yet all things subjected to him. But we behold him . . . crowned with glory and honour."

So, TO go back to our early illustrations of death which we too loosely called "the will of God," we can only admit them as God's circumstantial will. Somebody once asked me, when a baby had fallen out of a fifth-story window, whether its death was the will of God. The question shows how important it is that we should get our thinking straight, for the answer is both Yes and No. Yes, it is God's circumstantial will. I mean there that it is God's will that the law of gravity should operate. It is God's will that a baby is made of flesh and blood; and if a baby hits a concrete pavement after falling from such a height, of course it is God's will that the little body should be broken—otherwise God would have made babies' bodies of something like India rubber. Yet we feel that we must answer the question by an emphatic No and say that the death of the baby was not the will of God, for it was not the will of God that it should be allowed to fall out of the window at all.

Again and again, when people ask, "Is it the will of God?" I think we shall have to separate the subject in order to make an intelligent answer.

Consider, for example, the matter of disease. The Christian minister is continually confronted, as he does his visiting, by the question as to whether the onset of disease is the will of God. The important answer is No. The will of God for man is perfect health. Other things being equal, God can use a body free from disease more effectively than a diseased body. Jesus would not have been a greater spiritual asset in his early ministry if he had been lame or diabetic or tubercular. But there is a will of God within evil circumstances; and let every sufferer who may happen to read these lines realize that if he makes the right reaction to these circumstances, the ultimate will of God will be reached *as effectively as if*

27

*he had not been ill.* God would not allow cancer if *of itself* it had the power to defeat him.

The point may be seen, perhaps, by thinking of those diseases which are due to an invasion of germs. I suppose God is responsible for the creation of germs, even the germs of disease. Why they are created I don't know. It may be that they serve some good function about which we know nothing. It may be that they have served, in the evolutionary process, some good function. I don't think anybody knows the answer to that question. If these germs invade a body the resistance of which evil circumstances have lowered, then the result is disease; and that disease you can call, if you like, the circumstantial will of God. But it is the will of God only within the circumstances created by evil.

Here again let me repeat that that circumstantial will can be viewed from two angles—the first natural, the second spiritual. There is the physical condition which we call disease; but, second, there is the possibility of the patient's making such a splendid response to that circumstance that he creates out of it a spiritual asset in the community of much more value than most people's health. It is because the saints have thus reacted to evil that the fallacy has got about that disease and suffering are the will of God. Let me put it this way. Given a spiritual awakening so glorious that the personality lives in close co-operation with God, the healthy body is more in line with his will. But so many healthy people are spiritually asleep and are not co-operating with him at all, and so many sick people have, through the sickness, become spiritually awakened during their illness that out of the circumstances of evil they have created and set free spiritual energies far more valuable than the spiritual apathy of the healthy person.

I am quite sure that the battle *against* disease is the

will of God, and I thank God for all those people who are taking part in it. In olden days in this country, wolves used to descend from the woods upon a village and do a great deal of harm. But our sturdy forefathers did not call the invasion of the wolves "the will of God." They called up all their resources, and they "liquidated" the wolves. When the community is set upon by an invasion of germs, that is not the will of God. The situation is just the same. You may tell me that the animals are smaller and the germs of disease can be seen only through a microscope, but the problem is the same, and the battle is the same. I cannot understand how anybody who has read the New Testament can ever stand at the bedside of a patient and, without explaining himself, utter the pathetic complaint that disease is the will of God. I always imagine that Jesus would speak with anger about such a thoughtless dictum. When a woman was brought to him who had been ill for a long time, he spoke of her as "this woman . . . whom Satan hath bound, lo, these eighteen years." Satan! As far as I can understand Jesus' attitude, both in the words he spoke and the healing miracles he so gloriously wrought, he always regarded disease as part of the kingdom of evil, and with all his powers he fought it and instructed his followers to do the same.

I like to think of our Lord standing by the bedside of the patient and working with the doctors and nurses toward the regaining of health, working on the mind and spirit of the patient as the physicians work on the body. Then, if the latter fail, I like to think of him showing the sufferer that, in co-operation with him, victory may still be wrested from defeat and the purposes of God realized.

ONE final thought. If you say, "Well, it's a bit casual of God to *allow* these things to happen if they are not his intention," I agree that there is mystery there. It would be foolish to speak as if all the ways of God to men were clear. I should not like to give the impression that I could make a glib answer to any specific case of suffering that was brought to my notice. I too am often appalled at the suffering people endure, and especially little children.

Yet I wonder if, in a sense, we are not all in the position of little children. I can imagine a child looking up to his own father who loves him, and saying to him, "Don't you think you are rather casual to let me get hurt the way you do?" I amused myself, as I thought about this, by imagining a mass meeting of tiny toddlers who magically had the gift of putting their thoughts into words. Think of them, if you like, crowded into a great hall, with a little toddler as chairman, who, adjusting his bib, addresses his fellow toddlers in some such way as this: "I am sure my parents don't care. Look at my knees!" And there they were all red and scratched. And I imagined the meeting passing this resolution: "That this meeting protests against the carelessness of parents, and demands that in future no furniture shall be made with sharp corners, that gravel paths and hard playgrounds shall be abolished, and that claws shall be removed from the paws of all tame cats." I am sure the resolution would be passed unanimously. We do not say to God, "Look at my knees!" but we do say, "Look at my frustration and sorrow and disappointment and pain! How *can* you be so callous, and how *do* you expect us to think you care?" Perhaps childhood's tragedies are to us what our tragedies are to God—not that he is callous any more than the ideal parent is, but that his perspective is different. But the thought that comforts the child comforts me. If the child thought about it, I think he would say, "There is much I don't understand, but I know that my father both loves and cares." So,, for myself, I am quite certain that because God is love there is nothing in his world that can be regarded as meaningless torture. There is much I cannot understand. There must be much that I cannot be made to understand until I have passed out of childhood's stage. But because I know him through other means, and especially as revealed in Jesus, I know that although I cannot understand the answer to my questions, there *is* an answer, and in that I can rest content.

> I only know I cannot drift
> Beyond His love and care.

One cannot avoid being deeply impressed by the kind of answer Jesus gave when men came to him with their questions. When John the Baptist asked him a question, he said, "Suffer it to be so now." When Peter asked him a question, he said, "What I do thou knowest not now; but thou shalt know hereafter." And when, on the darkest night of the world's history, the night before his death, they all asked him questions, he said, "I have yet many things to say unto you, but ye cannot bear them now."

You see, even Jesus did not say, "I have explained the world." What he did say was, "I have overcome the world." And if we can only trust where we cannot see, walking in the light we have—which is often very much like hanging on in the dark—if we do faithfully that which we see to be the will of God in the circumstances which evil thrusts upon us, we can rest our minds in the assurance that circumstances which God allows, reacted to in faith and trust and courage, can never defeat purposes which God ultimately wills. So doing, we shall wrest from life something big and splendid. We shall find peace in our own hearts. We shall achieve integration in our own minds. We shall be able to serve our fellows with courage and joy. And then one day—for this has been promised us—we shall look up into his face and understand. Now we see in a mirror, darkly, but then face to face. Frankly, hard though it be to say so, it is a lack of faith not to be able to bear the thought of anything which God allows.

I know that right is right; that givers shall increase;
That duty lights the way for the beautiful feet of peace;
That courage is better than fear, and faith is truer than doubt.
And fierce though the fiends may fight, and long though the
    angels hide,
I know that Truth and Right have the Universe on their side;
And that somewhere beyond the stars is a Love that is
    stronger than hate;
When the night unlocks her bars, I shall see Him—and I
    will wait.

# 3

## GOD'S
## ULTIMATE WILL

THERE IS A SENTENCE AT THE END OF THE BOOK of Job which summarizes the message of this section: "I know that thou canst do all things, and that no purpose of thine can be restrained"—or, as Moffatt translates it, "Nothing is too hard for thee."

We have spoken of the intentional will of God—that is, God's original plan for the well-being of his children, an intention spoiled by man's folly and sin. We have spoken of God's circumstantial will, his will within the circumstances set up by man's evil. I want to write here of God's ultimate will, the goal which I believe he reaches, not only *in spite of* all man may do, but even using man's evil to further his own plan.

Turning to the Cross once more as the supreme example, we see again that—

1. The intentional will of God was not that Jesus should be crucified, but that he should be followed;

2. The circumstantial will of God, God's will in the circumstances which men's evil provided, was that Jesus should accept death, but accept it in such a positive and creative way as to lead to

3. God's ultimate will—namely, the redemption of man, winning man back to God, not in spite of the Cross, but using the Cross, born of man's sin, as an instrument to reach the goal of God's ultimate will.

33

The picture in my mind is that of children playing beside a tiny stream that runs down a mountainside to join a river in the valley below. Very little children can divert the stream and get great fun out of damming it up with stones and earth. But not one of them ever succeeds in preventing the water from reaching the river at last. (Don't press the illustration and remind me that the Royal Engineers could do so!) In regard to God we are very little children. Though we may divert and hinder his purposes, I don't believe we ever finally defeat them; and, though the illustration doesn't carry us so far, frequently our mistakes and sins are used to make another channel to carry the water of God's plans to the river of his purpose.

The omnipotence of God, you perceive, does not mean that by a sheer exhibition of his superior might God gets his own way. If he did, man's freedom would be an illusion and man's moral development would be made impossible. No "end" which God has in mind can be imposed from without; for his end, the at-one-ment of all souls with him, must come from man's choice of God's way, not the imposition of God's will in irresistible might which leaves no room for choice. Power means ability to achieve purpose. Since the purpose is to win man's volition, any activity of God's which denied or suppressed man's volition, in that it would defeat the purpose, would not be a use of power but a confession of weakness and an acceptance of defeat.

When we say, then, that God is omnipotent, we do not mean that nothing can happen unless it is God's will (= intention). We mean that nothing can happen which can *finally* defeat him.

If man is to have a real freedom, and if the community is to be bound together in such a close unity that the one suffers for the many, even as the one gains through the

34

many—if, in a word, life is to be on the family and not on the individual basis, then obviously ten thousand things can happen that God did not intend, and millions of innocent people will suffer through the sins of others. Of this great truth we need no far-fetched illustration. The horror of war and the suffering of innocent people prove it with terrible convincingness.

What is meant by the omnipotence of God is that he will reach at last his ultimate goal, that nothing of value will be lost in the process, however man may divert and dam up the stream of purpose nearest him, and that God —if he cannot use men as his agents—will, though with great pain to himself and to themselves, use them as his instruments. "I know that thou canst do all things, and that no purpose of thine can be restrained."

HERE is an illustration which may help. Many years ago there was no such thing as blotting paper. Ink was dried by dusting the page with a light powder. One day in a paper mill one of the workers made a mistake. Let us for the sake of argument say that he committed a sin. Through gross carelessness and inattention to duty he omitted a certain chemical or material, and the result was that the paper was entirely unfitted for writing material. The owner of the mill was angry. It looked as if the mistake meant the sheer loss of the whole material concerned. But when the paper was brought to him and he tried to write on it, he noticed the way the ink was immediately absorbed, and the idea of blotting paper occurred to him. Let us suppose, for the sake of the argument, that the goal of the mill owner was to make money. Then we see that apparent loss was turned to gain. The ultimate end (to make money) was reached when the intention (to make money from writing paper) was defeated and the circumstance thrown up by evil (the worker's careless inattention) was reacted to in a positive and creative way.

Of course no illustration we can devise covers all the ground. From this you might argue, "Very well then, let us not bother what we do, however stupid and careless and sinful we may be. If God can use evil as well as good, let him get on with it. Nothing we do matters."

But here is the old argument which Paul fought with such strength in his Epistle to the Romans. When men said, "Shall we continue in sin, that grace may abound?" he said, "God forbid. We who died to sin, how shall we any longer live therein?" Once we see what sin is—"the raised hand, the clenched fist, the blow in the face of God," as Joseph Parker called it—how can we practice it? It would be like a medical student smashing his mother's head with an ax and saying, "What of it? I have increased my knowledge of the structure of the brain." Sin is the blackest thing in the universe. It is one thing to say, "This evil has been done. How can I win good from it?" It is another thing to say, "I will deliberately do evil in order to win good from it."

Further, though God may *use* an instrument for the achievement of divine purpose, if that instrument is human, he has to pay for his sins. God *used* the Cross, we said, as the instrument of a divine purpose, but that did not stop our Lord from saying of Judas, "It had been good for that man if he had not been born," and again, "It must needs be that offences come; but woe to that man by whom the offence cometh!"

With this clear in our minds, however, the message comes to me in these days with immense comfort. These are days full of loss and pain, of suffering and sorrow. *But they are not days of waste.* They are the fruit of the whole world's sin. To go back to the blotting paper illustration, here is the work of slackness on the part not of one worker but of millions. We will not go back in thought with sentences that begin, "If only in 1918 we had . . ." That is too painful now. The result of that slackness is not wasted paper, but wasted lives, wasted homes, wasted cities, wasted money, wasted energy. But will it be waste? My answer is a ringing No! for the simple reason that I trust the Owner of this great mill of a world that is grinding out his purposes. He doesn't lose his temper and say of this world, "I'm sick of you. I wish I'd never created you."

Gash the earth with your railway cutting, and nature at once gets busy on the scar and covers it with not only the kind of green grass which grew on the surrounding fields but with tender violets and primroses which would not grow until a cleft in the earth provided shelter from the north wind. With evil intent men crucified the Son of God, and within six weeks other men were preaching about the Cross as the instrument of salvation. They hardly once referred to it as the crime of man. They— with a daring almost alarming—spoke of it as a redemptive act of God.

Now the whole world is crucified. But look what is happening! There is a new social conscience. What's all this talk about an education act, about new health provisions, new housing, new city planning? Why, what has that to do with war? There were slums before the war, and bad education and inadequate health provision. War hasn't made them. I tell you that the Spirit of God is at his glorious task. He is making the wrath of man to serve him and further his ultimate will. He is using the moment when men's hearts are awestruck at the horror their own evil has brought upon them, to rouse them to what has always been God's will, so that, awakened and responding, they may, through doing God's circumstantial will, reach his ultimate will as certainly as it would have been reached if his intentional will had been done. For surely the extreme horror of war was not necessary before men could understand God's intention for his children who live in great cities.

A YOUNG woman, widowed in an accident, says to me, "Yes, I can see your point in regard to world affairs and civic facilities, but come down to the individual. My man has been killed, and my two little children are left father-less, and I'm young, and life stretches on in an infinite loneliness. How can God ever reach in my life his ulti-mate will? His intentional will was surely home and married happiness. His will is defeated forever."

If I offered you a glib answer to that, I should hate myself and you would despise me. I set down the question because I want to be honest and not evade it. And here no one can answer save in faith, for no one can see the end from the beginning. Let me tenderly say one or two things. On Good Friday night eleven men, in the deepest gloom felt like you. They said in their hearts: "We trusted him, we followed him. It was his will to establish his kingdom. He told us so. And evil has been allowed to take him from us. It's the end of everything."

But they were wrong, weren't they? It was only the end of their mistake and the beginning of the most won-derful use of evil which God has ever effected. And if you give way to despair, you are wrong too! And one day, like them, you'll find out how wrong you are *and be sadder at your despair than at your loss.*

For you know your loved one is not lost. He is alive. He is working out a plan. And God is still using him in his plan. Maybe from the other side he's helping you. Can you take up life bravely in spiritual communion with the one you've lost? Can you be father and mother to your little ones? Can you comfort weaker hearts than

your own in this dark night of the world? Can you say
to yourself with Tennyson

> That nothing walks with aimless feet;
> That not one life shall be destroy'd,
> Or cast as rubbish to the void,
> When God hath made the pile complete?

If so, I'm certain you won't be defrauded, that all will be
woven into the pattern, that when you get to the end of
the road you will not feel any sense of injustice or any
sense of loss. God's intentional will was the fulfillment
of your personality via what we might call the mountain
stream of years of married life. That stream is now
blocked. Are you certain, standing where you stand, with
your limited human vision, that God cannot fulfill your
personality by any other route? Big words these, but
underneath them is the conviction of all the saints and
the supreme evidence of the Crucified that God is a
Father, that the ultimate meaning of the whole universe
is Love, and that God will never fail with one of his
family unless that one opposes him forever.

Evil can do terrible things to us. The more I read and
think, the more I believe in a Devil. "God lets the Devil
have a long rope these days," said a friend of mine, a
doctor of divinity, to his mother. "Yes," said the old lady,
"but he keeps hold of the end of it himself." God still
reigns—a God who is like Jesus, who died to make a
dream come true that is better than our wildest dreams.
Rest in this thought about God's ultimate will. "Eye hath
not seen, nor ear heard, neither have entered into the
heart of man, the things which God hath prepared for
them that love him." Trust God. Rest in the nature of
God. He who began this strange adventure we call
human life will also control the end. "I am Alpha and

*Omega,* the beginning and the *end,* the first and the *last.*" The last word is with God—

> That God, which ever lives and loves,
> One God, one law, one element,
> And one far-off divine event,
> To which the whole creation moves—

"one far-off divine event" whose nature no man may dream, but which we may call the accomplishment of the ultimate will of God.

# 4

## DISCERNING THE WILL OF GOD

HAVING MADE THE FOREGOING DISTINCTIONS IN REGARD to the will of God, we may inquire now whether it can be discerned by us and how. My mental picture for you is that of a man lost in a wood. We need not decide whether it is his own fault that he is lost, or whether he has been misdirected, or whether he has been the victim of some accident. He is asking a question which has often been on people's lips lately: "Where do I go from here?" He feels that there must be a path which is the path of God's will for him in those circumstances, but how can he be sure it is God's way, and how can he be certain that he won't make a mistake?

Let me answer the last question first. To be quite honest he cannot be *certain* until he gets to the end that he won't make a mistake, for he must travel by faith more than by sight. But if he is willing to read the signposts and follow them, he will come out to the place where God wants him to be; and, fortunately, God deals with us where we are. There is an amusing story of a motorist who leaned out of his car and asked a yokel the way to York. The yokel replied, "Well, sir, if I were going to York, I shouldn't start from here." Fortunately God can start with us where we are, and he has ways of showing us the path of his will.

41

I am quite sure that the greatest help available in discerning the will of God is reached when we deepen our friendship with him. Those who know God are the quickest and surest at discerning his will. Sometimes you will hear men and women in conference discussing a gift which they wish to make to an absent member. Then perhaps someone will say, "Well, I have known him for fifty years. I know what he would like us to do"; and I think, generally speaking, the authority is recognized. Sometimes in interpreting a dead man's will we hear someone say, "I know what he would have liked best"; and knowledge and friendship and love become a qualification for deciding what would be the wishes of the person concerned.

Surely it was the friendship Jesus had with God—if we may call it by so simple a word—that made him so utterly certain at every twist and turn of the tortuous road he trod as to which direction was the will of God. He *almost* lost his way in the Garden; the night was very dark. It was hard to find the way; but, kneeling there in agony of mind, with his magic key—"Nevertheless not what I will, but what thou wilt"—he opened the door that led to death, believing that in those circumstances he must take the path of the Cross.

But, friendship apart, there are numerous signposts which give us some direction, and I would like to speak of them briefly.

1. Conscience may be of lowly origin. Some people think it is a kind of group wisdom gathered through the ages as men found out that some ways of living led to a precipice, and some to a dead end, and some were truly thoroughfares. I know that much scorn can be poured on this lowly voice within our hearts. Men have done evil believing that they followed the dictates of conscience.

The voice is distorted by the spiritual level the race has reached and depends on the sensibility of the one who responds to it. Even men of the same generation differ here. One can do things without a qualm of conscience, while another, doing the same thing, would bring himself into a torment of remorse, and it may not necessarily be that either is justified by the facts. For years slavery was uncondemned by the consciences of men, and centuries ahead it will be incredible that our consciences could sleep about slums and war. But when all this has been said, we all recognize a voice that says, "This is right; that is wrong," and that the path of God's will is the former.

2. Then there is the lowly signpost we call "common sense." "I prayed for advice," said a man once, "but nothing happened, and I got no answer to my prayers; so I used my common sense." But who gave him his common sense, and why was it given? If God has placed the machinery for making a judgment within the mind of man, why should he not use it, and why should man regard some uncanny way of receiving direction as more likely to be divine because it is unusual? Surely insight based on a thoughtful appreciation of the situation is more reliable than impulse. At the same time a warning must be uttered, in that sometimes the direction of the will of God is the opposite of that which common sense would dictate. The will of God is sometimes what the world would call "madness."

3. Let us not disregard the value of the advice of a friend. I do not mean the counsel of a professional minister or consultant, but talking over one's difficulties with a wise friend who, because he can see the matter from a different angle, can view the pros and cons dispassionately and, because he is outside the emotional setting of the problem, can often give us the most helpful advice. Of

course there are some problems where God's best way of helping us is through the advice of the expert. In a difficult medical or psychological situation we may not have enough knowledge to obtain the maximum wisdom without the expert who has made the field of our particular difficulty his own special study. But here again let us think of the adviser as an instrument God can use, just as he can use our own judgment. Remember two quotations from Browning:

> Hush, I pray you!
> What if this friend happen to be—God?

and again:

> God teaches us to help each other so,
> Lending our minds out.

Get a friend with Christian insight to lend you his mind in your problem, and God will direct you. I don't mean to imply a necessary identification of what the friend advises with what God wills, but a new angle on your problem will help you to see the latter more clearly.

4. There is another way of using the minds and wisdom of others. We reach it as we read great literature, especially biography and history. Again and again it has been to me of inexpressible comfort to read the biographies of great men. Very few problems there are in our lives which great men and women have not had to face before us; and when we read the Bible, which is a library of every kind of literature, but literature all written from a unique point of view—that of the will and purposes of God—then perhaps most clearly of all are we allowed to share in the guidance which God gives his children as they seek to discern his will.

5. Not enough is made, I feel, of the voice of the Church. Jesus once strongly recommended to people to consult the Church. (Matt. 18:17.) I feel that it is not too strong a thing to say that no church is functioning as it ought to do unless there are fellowship groups in it to which the puzzled member may bring his own problem. He may, indeed, disguise it, saying, "I know a man who . . . ," when the man is himself. But I can say from experience at the City Temple that sometimes direction to a troubled soul who seeks to discern the will of God has come with crystal clearness when a group of detached, thoughtful, loving Christian people has been asked what the mind of God is, and what the will of God is, in a certain situation laid before it.

6. Our Quaker friends make much of what they call "Inner Light," and I entirely support the claims they make. They say that God can speak directly to the human soul and show his will to those who seek him. This is undoubtedly true. I would utter only one word of caution. To follow the practice of the Oxford Groups, to endeavor to blank the mind and then take whatever comes into that mind as the will of God, is fraught with a great danger. We are liable to fall into the fallacy of supposing that the method by which we receive this "light" makes it divine, but the thought or impulse that comes to the blank mind is just as much the fruit of earlier mental processes as is, for instance, the thought that comes to the mind after a long argument. Actually one cannot blank the mind or disengage it at any point from all that has gone before. It is as impossible as isolating a wave of the sea and supposing that it has no relation to the waves behind it and the waves before it. Yet if the method is used with wisdom and caution, and if what "comes" in the quiet time is tested by some other ways indicated above or, as the Groupers say, "checked up"

with others, no one who knows the facts would deny that God's will is often discerned in this way.

IN these ways, then, the will of God, at the point at which we need help, may be discerned. Let me underline that last phrase—*at the point at which we need help.* Sometimes I have made a mistake myself by trying to discern the will of God for years ahead. I have come to the conclusion that God does not encourage us to see too far ahead. One simply must accept the fact that one has no idea where the road one is treading is going to lead. Suffice it to say that when one gets to the crossroads one will know which way to turn, and although we like to think that it is terribly important not to make a mistake —and I repeat one can never be certain that one has not made a mistake—yet I adhere earnestly to the view expressed in the section on the ultimate will of God. Our mistakes, if made in good faith, will not result in our being lost. "We shall not miss our providential way." God often wonderfully weaves mistakes into his plan, as he also weaves our sufferings and our sins.

Let me end this section, however, with two challenging questions which I put to myself and would pass on to you.

1. Do I really want to discern God's will, or do I want to get his sanction for my own? An amusing story is told of a minister who was invited to a church at which the salary was four times what he was already receiving; and, being a devout man, he spent many hours in prayer seeking to discern the will of God. One day a friend met the minister's little boy in the street and said, "Well, what is your father going to do?"

"Well," said the little boy, "Father's praying, but Mother's packing."

The father was saying to God, "What wilt thou have

me to do?" and the mother, no less good-intentioned, was saying to God, "This is what I am going to do. I hope you will approve."

Discerning the will of God does really mean putting ourselves out of the picture—not choosing a way as his because it is unpleasant (we have dealt already with that fallacy), but certainly not going to the other extreme and saying, "This is what I am going to do. Please approve, because I want so badly to do it."

2. The second challenging question is this: Have I got the courage to do God's will when I discern it? Many people ask a great many questions as to how they may find the will of God, and every minister knows what it is to sit down with an inquiring person in order to find out the answer to the question. But most ministers have also had experience of those people who, seeing clearly the will of God, say, "No, anything but that." It is only because I see this weakness in myself that I would pass on to others the warning that usually what one needs is not discernment but grit. For myself, more than I need discernment I need fortitude, courage, faith, determination, and perseverance. Not to see, merely, but to do. As Drinkwater puts it:

Knowledge we ask not—knowledge Thou hast lent,
But, Lord, the will—there lies our bitter need,
Give us to build above the deep intent
    The deed, the deed.

# 5

## "IN HIS WILL
## IS OUR PEACE"

IN THIS SECTION I SHOULD LIKE THE READER TO HAVE
in his mind not only the sentence of Dante which
stands at the head, "In his will is our peace," but also a
word of God for us in the book of Proverbs: "In all thy
ways acknowledge him, and he shall direct thy paths."

We may feel that it was all very well for Dante to
say, "In his will is our peace"; but there are so many
things happening in the world to-day that are outside his
will—at any rate in the sense of being outside his intention—that we may feel debarred from peace. Exactly!
That is why we do not find peace, but instead war without and restlessness within. After all the years of war it
is not surprising to find so many people ill. If not in-
capacitated in body, thousands are anxious and worried
and sleepless. But on top of it, if a man has any imagina-
tion or sensitiveness left, and lets his mind brood over the
slaughter and suffering, the worry and unhappiness of
this war-stricken world, his mind is continually wounded,
and the power of the mind over the body is so great that
one almost feels it is true to say that only those can feel
well who are living, both mentally and physically, remote
from the horror of war, or who somehow, by virtue of
their temperament or their indifference or by the skillful
practice of looking the other way, have built up a wall of

defense between themselves and the bleeding world around them. For most of us there is the dull sorrow which goes on day after day, and which then is suddenly focused into some poignant case of suffering, thrusting itself upon our attention because the sufferer is dear to us, or because he chooses us as the recipient of his burden. One is glad when he finds the relief of a burden shared, but sometimes some of us feel we do not know how to go on for another day. We are so burdened down that we even feel impatient with Dante, and say, "Yes, but all this is not his will, and therefore how may peace be found?"

Here should come, I think, the value of our earlier thinking and our distinction between the intentional, the circumstantial, and the ultimate will of God.

We saw that even though the intentional will of God is deflected by man's misuse of free will—by the folly and ignorance in the world, and by that family relationship through which all humanity is so closely bound together that your sins affect me and my sins hurt you—yet, even so, there is *a* will of God within the circumstances which evil has caused. I believe, as we have said before, that the Cross was not the intention of God for Jesus. God's intention was that Jesus should be followed, not crucified. But when evil men thrust the Cross upon him, he accepted God's will in those circumstances and so reacted to them that he made his Cross an instrument of power by which the ultimate will of God could be done. In the Garden of Gethsemane, when the shadows were falling upon him, he saw, like Bunyan's pilgrim, the bright Light; and by keeping on the path that led to it, he achieved God's purposes not only in spite of the Cross, but through it.

So the message of this section is that no evil circumstances can ever befall us but we can find in them a path

which is God's way for us just then, and we must train
ourselves, as we saw in the last section, so to discern the
will of God that we shall not falter or fail to find the path.
When we find it, then, though all the world is in tumult,
there is at least an inner peace at the core of our being
—a peace that comes from knowing that we are within
his will and his will is revealed to us in those circumstances and at that moment.

To BE within God's will means peace for three reasons:
1. We lose the fear of getting lost. Everyone knows
the terror of the child who cannot find the path that
leads to home. There is a good illustration for us here in
the way an airman finds his way home. A radio beam is
sent out from his own home station, and once in that
beam he has only to follow it to find his way. If he goes
out of that directing beam a buzzer sounds in his ear-
phones, telling him clearly enough: "You are going
wrong. You must get back until all is quiet." In the home
beam there is peace. I think it is not stretching the illustration to say that God sends out, as it were, a beam of
direction—namely, his will for us in those circumstances
in which we find ourselves—and as long as we keep in
his will there is peace. It is when we go out of it or cannot find it—and this can be our case sometimes, however
hard we try, as I know to my sorrow—that disturbance
and unrest are set up in our minds.

I suspect that the same thing happens in the brain of
a bird. We must not talk of the "courage" and "trust" of
the swallow, for these are values which have no meaning
in birdland. But in the spring or early summer a swallow
away in Africa will start off on a journey of thousands of
miles, and come back to the eaves of the same little
village church among the elms where she built her nest
last year. She will not be deflected or lose her way. She

will find an unknown path through storms and driving winds and across the leagues of sea without disturbance, fretting, or anxiety, because, although mechanically, she is in the path of God's will, and in his will there is peace. So, says Browning:

> I go to prove my soul!
> I see my way as birds their trackless way.
> I shall arrive! what time, what circuit first,
> I ask not. . . .
> In some time, his good time, I shall arrive.

Let us take this message to heart, that by keeping within the will of God, as we see it in any experience, we find our way even through apparently overwhelming storms, until we arrive at last where God wants us to be —and the goal of all human endeavor is to fulfill God's purposes and to be one with him.

2. The second reason why I think we find peace within the will of God is this: The dread of carrying the responsibility of what happens is removed. What a dreadful moment it was when the crowd, intent on the crucifixion of Christ, shouted out: "His blood be on us, and on our children." They were asserting that they were quite ready to take the responsibility for their actions. It is that responsibility which so often weighs us down. But I believe God's message to us includes this: it is as though he said, "As long as you try to do my will, I will accept responsibility for whatever happens. I will carry that burden for you. I will direct you, and the consequences are my responsibility, not yours." "In all thy ways acknowledge him, and he shall direct thy paths."

Perhaps an illustration will serve here. I heard recently of a little girl whose mother was away from home, so that the child had the task of housekeeping for her father and several smaller brothers or sisters. One can only imagine the burden of responsibility which the child carried, as she tried to fill her mother's place, not only in keeping house, but in answering the demands of the smaller children. She bore up bravely and carried through her duties splendidly, but when her mother came back, one can imagine the relief of the little girl as she cried, "Oh, Mummy, I'm so glad you have come." Remember that the child probably still did most of the duties that she had been doing before, but her mother bore the responsibility. I feel that the illustration goes a good way, that when we submit our will to the will of God, in a sense we can say to God, "I'm so glad you have come." We are not any longer carrying out a set of duties in loneliness and bearing the responsibility of life alone. We are trying to do the will of One who is all the time there, and who says to us: "All you have to do is to follow the plan of my will from day to day, and the responsibility for what happens I will carry for you." Instead of that we are trying to bear in the world what is God's burden of responsibility.

I wonder if I might further illustrate by quoting part of a prayer which I wrote down for my own comfort recently, during some very heavy days of strain:

Lord Jesus, Bearer of men's burdens, Comforter of the sorrowful, we would bring to thee all whose hearts are sad. Help us to mediate thy strengthening sympathy to others, but grant that we may be so continually refreshed by our companionship with thee that we may not be crushed by the world's burdens. Thou art the burden bearer—not we. Thou art the Redeemer—not we. Thou alone, O Christ, canst in thy strong heart carry the woes of the world. In this faith, teach us to do our duty day by day as we see it to be thy will, and save us from the depression of those who try to carry more than man was made to bear, and ever to

look to thee, O Lamb of God who bearest the sins of the
world.

3. The third reason why God's will means our peace
is that in his will our conflicts are resolved. I am aware
that an element of conflict is essential to the progress of
the soul. The soul that is unconscious of any conflict
would be one ceasing to recognize a clash of good and
evil—the soul so dulled by acquiescence to impulse that
temptation had lost its power, the thing desired being
done without conflict. A dreadful deterioration of personality would follow. At the same time, how weak is the
man who constantly weighs "Shall I do this?" with
"Shall I do that?" The guiding principle "I will do
God's will as far as I can see it" is one that answers a
great many of our conflicts and therefore brings us peace
and strength. If it be said, "Yes, but you could end conflict by deciding to do wrong," my answer is that doing
wrong always sets up a dozen conflicts where formerly
there was one. We wade more and more deeply into the
morass of evil and are exhausted in the attempts to get
out of it, for the trend of the universe is toward goodness.

> For the everlasting right
> The eternal stars are strong.

If this were a psychological lecture, I should try to
explain how often the personality is exhausted by these
conflicts. As I write these words, I recall a young officer
in the A.T.S. who once consulted me, complaining of a
fatigue so great that at times she could not lift her arms
above shoulder level in order to do her hair. Her mind
was tormented by the obsession that she would fall ill.
The truth was that part of her mind wanted to fall ill
because illness would bring sympathy, love, the security

of home, and her parents' care. A recent love affair which had been broken off had deprived her of love, and she craved the love of her mother. But another part of her mind feared illness, since illness in her case, for which there was no real cause, would only be a guilt-causing get-out from the Army life that she hated and in which there was no chance of being loved. The hunger for love and the deprivation of love are known to every psychologist as fruitful causes of neurosis.

Again and again these conflicts weaken and exhaust us. A young girl feels the conflict between duty to her mother and a desire for independence. Dr. Hadfield tells us that in the mind of a soldier the sense of duty was so much in conflict with the desire to run away, promoted by the self-preservation instinct, that a condition of paralysis of the legs was produced which solved the immediate problem but of course disabled the patient. In our own psychological clinic I have known the conflict in a student between the desire to excel, as he had done at school, and the inferiority which he felt so keenly when proceeding to the university, where he found himself among those of finer mental caliber than he had met at school. The frustration of not being, as it were, top of the class any longer, the fear of being found out to be ordinary, and the desire for the top places even in the university produced a conflict so exhausting as to disable the patient altogether. Hadfield wisely says: "By facing our conflicts and deliberately making our choice, by directing all our endeavors to one great purpose, confidently and fearlessly, the soul is restored to harmony and strength."

I always imagine that the lovely picture Jesus painted in his phrase, "Take my yoke upon you, and learn of me; for I am meek and lowly in heart: and ye shall find rest unto your souls," is really that of the strong ox yoked with the weaker, untried animal. The weaker has to pull

54

only his own weight, as we say, and keep level with the stronger. The stronger carries the heavy end of the yoke. The stronger is responsible for the straight furrow and for reaching the end of it. If the weaker keeps pulling out into a direction of his own, the yoke chafes his shoulders, and the burden becomes heavy. "Take my yoke upon you," says Jesus, "and learn of me to be meek and lowly in heart. Don't be self-opinionated and proud and self-assertive, saying, 'I'm going my own way.' By doing that you make the yoke chafe your shoulders. Walk with me, and it becomes easy (in the true sense of that word). The responsibility is taken from you, and the burden becomes light." "In his will is our peace."

In my early teens I often had a holiday at a farmhouse in the Charnwood Forest. Near the farm there was one rocky crag on which I loved to sit, especially at sunset hour. Below my feet the hillside ran steeply down to a big reservoir, fringed with reeds and rushes. Then there was the expanse of water, and on the other side of it a grand red granite crag, rising sheer from the lake and crowned with stately pines. I have sat there in silence at all hours of the day. I can close my eyes now and recover the sense of calm and peace that came to me in that lonely spot. I can almost hear the cry of the coot in the rushes, the lovely whisper of the wind in the bracken, and the chattering of the water among the stones of a tiny beach between the reeds. One day there came to me, almost as a revelation, a thought which may be quite a platitude to you, but which struck my mind with the shock of truth. There was no human being or even human habitation in sight. Everything I could see was fulfilling perfectly the will of God. Agreed that that will was mechanically done and that the wild life around me had no burden of choice, but I seemed to learn the secret of

the harmony and peace of that spot. The will of God was
perfectly done. If we could do voluntarily that which is
done in nature mechanically, I believe we should find
the same sense of peace. "In all thy ways acknowledge
him [as the birds do], and he shall direct thy paths."

The poets say these things better than we do. Let me
conclude with some verses of the poet William Cullen
Bryant, written as he watched the figure of a wild bird
flying, as it seemed, into the heart of the sunset:

> Whither, 'midst falling dew,
> While glow the heavens with the last steps of day,
> Far, through their rosy depths, dost thou pursue
> Thy solitary way?
>
> Vainly the fowler's eye
> Might mark thy distant flight to do thee wrong,
> As, darkly painted on the crimson sky,
> Thy figure floats along.
>
> Seek'st thou the plashy brink
> Of weedy lake, or marge of river wide,
> Or where the rocking billows rise and sink
> On the chafed ocean side?
>
> There is a Power whose care
> Teaches thy way along that pathless coast,—
> The desert and illimitable air,—
> Lone wandering, but not lost.
>
> Thou'rt gone, the abyss of heaven
> Hath swallowed up thy form; yet, on my heart
> Deeply hath sunk the lesson thou hast given,
> And shall not soon depart.
>
> He who, from zone to zone,
> Guides through the boundless sky thy certain flight,
> In the long way that I must tread alone
> Will lead my steps aright.

56